A 40 MINUTE
DAILY DOSE OF
MAINTENANCE
AND
DEVELOPMENT
FOR TRUMPET

Published by CFM PUBLICATIONS

ISBN-13: 978-1726381840
ISBN-10: 1726381846

About the Author

Jazz artist Craig Fraedrich has enjoyed a professional career as a performer and educator that spans over thirty years. He received his undergraduate degree in Jazz Performance from North Texas State University and Masters Degree from Arizona State University. He also studied at the University of Wisconsin-Milwaukee and the Banff Center for the Arts. He was awarded music scholarships at each of these institutions. While in college he won numerous solo awards at jazz festivals throughout the country including: The Elmhurst Jazz Festival, The Notre Dame Jazz Festival, The Wichita Jazz Festival, The UT-Austin Jazz Festival, The University of Arizona – Flagstaff Jazz Festival and the University of California – Berklee Jazz Festival where he was named the outstanding soloist of the Festival. He was a winner of International Trumpet Guild Jazz Solo competition and leader/director of the first student combo to perform at the International Jazz Educators Conference.

From 1986-2017 he performed as a featured jazz trumpet soloist with The Army Blues, the premier jazz ensemble of the United States Army and one of the few full-time jazz ensembles in the country. During that time he also served as the group's musical director, trumpet section leader, assistant group leader and Group Leader. In addition to performing, he composed or arranged over 100 pieces for the band. As a member of this prestigious ensemble, Craig has traveled extensively both performing and serving as a clinician. In addition to visiting much of the United States, he has performed in Australia, Japan, Sweden, Norway, Germany, China, Ireland, St. Thomas and at the Montreux Jazz Festival in Switzerland. He finished his career as a Sergeant Major, serving as the leader of the Army Blues and Element Leader of the Popular Music Element.

Craig has pursued a significant solo career as well. He has released twelve compact discs with his own groups and has appeared on dozens of others as a side-man. His release, *So In Love* (featuring NEA Jazz Master Dave Liebman) reached number twelve in national jazz radio play according to Billboard Magazine. His two most recent releases, *All Through the Night* (2017) on Summit Records and *Out Of the Blues* (2018) on CFM Recordings both enjoyed substantial national radio play and remain available. Other performance highlights have included an appearance as guest jazz soloist with the Brass Band of Battle Creek for the premier of Wycliff Gordon's **"Tribute to Muhammad Ali"** as well as the Kennedy Center's presentation of Ramsey Lewis's **"Proclamation of Hope"**, both of which were recorded for PBS. Craig continues to maintain a busy schedule in the Washington D.C. area. He is a dedicated educator and has been a faculty member (Associate Professor) at the Shenandoah Conservatory of Music since 1989 and was a Lecturer at West Virginia

University from 2013 to 2016. His duties have included: teaching Applied Jazz Trumpet, Jazz Coaching (applied jazz lessons for any instrument) Music Theory, Jazz Theory, Jazz Arranging and Composition, Jazz Improvisation, Jazz Combos, the Little Big Band and has been the director of the Shenandoah Jazz Ensemble since 1999. Highlights directing the Jazz Ensemble included tours of Senegal West Africa with performances culminating at the St. Louis Jazz Festival and a tour of Ireland with a featured performance at the National Concert Hall.

Craig has published three books as part of the ***Practical Jazz Theory for Improvisation*** series as well as ***A Daily Dose of Scales for Improvisation*** in treble and bass clef versions. He has studied improvisation with Dave Liebman, Kenny Wheeler, Chuck Marohnic, Rich Matteson, Dan Hearle, Jack Peterson, and Frank Puzzullo. Additionally, he cites the remaining faculty at the Banff Centre for the Arts (1985- Dave Holland, John Abercrombie, Don Thompson, Marvin "Smitty" Smith, and Julian Priester) as major influences. His principal trumpet teachers have included Dennis Najoom, Dr. Leonard Candelaria, Don Jacoby, Dr. Wayne Cook, Steve Kossoris, Chuck Tumlinson and Ken Van Winkle.

About This Book

The value of this text lies primarily in the organization and adaptation of well-understood developmental approaches into a manageable daily maintenance routine. As written, it requires a significant level of development to fully accomplish. The ability to play it through as written likely implies a player who has already spent significant time with one or more of great development methods such as: Claude Gordon, Stamp, Maggio, Caruso, Reinhardt, etc. That being said, by skipping portions that exceed a student's ability, this book could be used as a developmental method and precursor to study using any one of the above-mentioned texts.

There are several potential ways to approach this routine. The first is as a warm-up/initial practice session of the day. This approach includes a recommendation of at least an hour (preferably longer) break prior to any performance or rehearsal as it is strenuous. The second is to divide the routine in half, using sections 1-3 as a warm-up and returning to sections 4-6 later in the day. This is particularly useful if sections 1-3 prove to be an adequate and effective warm-up for an individual. The third would be to do the routine as the last session of the day. Many players find it advantageous to do developmental/maintenance work as the last work of the day – especially if they already have a warm-up that they find effective and has proven successful. In this case, spending some additional time on the chromatic and low C to pedal C exercises as a warm-down might help the following morning's warm-up.

One of the elements that aids the effectiveness of this routine is the alternation of embouchure stressing exercises with embouchure relaxing exercises – primarily chromatics adapted from Herbert L. Clarke's *Technical Studies* and pedal tones adapted primarily from Claude Gordon's *Systematic Approach to Daily Practice*. For anyone who has previously worked with any of the methods mentioned above, (Claude Gordon, Stamp, Maggio, Caruso, Reinhardt, etc.) the pedal tones here should not be new. For anyone who has not, as of this writing, a simple search of the internet and *YouTube* provides multiple explanations, demonstrations and techniques for pedal tones on trumpet. Virtually any of them would provide a good introduction to getting started. As technique with pedal tones develops and provided the jaw isn't dropped too far, movement of the tongue while descending in the pedal range should mirror movement while ascending above high C.

The marked metronome ranges are suggested. With the exception of the chromatics, the exercises provide greatest benefit when played in the slower ranges. Exercises should be played at a dynamic of *mp–mf* as appropriate.

The **Section 1 Coordination** exercise is an excellent way to begin the day. Relax between each note, approaching each as a distinct and separate attack with a focus on relaxation and free flow of air. The low C to pedal C exercise without valves is important and is repeated throughout the text. Focus on finding the shape of each pitch by moving your tongue up and forward and avoid dropping the jaw.

The **Section 2 Long Tones** are more challenging as the tempo decreases. A comfortable tempo that allows for completion to start is recommended. If using the first 3 sections as a warm-up prior to a rehearsal or performance, a slightly faster tempo is recommended.

The **Section 3 Flow** exercises here are adaptations of the well-known Vincent Chicowitz *Flow Studies*. They have been altered from the original to include an important slurred major triad from the tonic and in this context, are intended to be played at least twice as fast as is traditional with the original Chicowitz exercises. They should be played as connected as possible, with a full but not loud sound, and at as steady a volume as possible. The marked dynamic of *mp–mf* refers to a consistent dynamic with only the slightest crescendo ascending in order to maintain a full sound and free flow of air. If either exercise **3-7** or **3-10** ascends too high to start, reversing the order and playing systems from the bottom of the page to the top is acceptable. No more than three attempts should be taken to successfully play any given system.

Section 4 extends range both downward into the pedal range as well upward, connecting the pedal range to the upper register. The pedal tones using valves in exercise **4-1** should be much easier and produce a bigger sound than playing the low C to pedal C all open. Suggested valve combinations are provided, but are not the only options. While the jaw might drop some while descending, the less the better. Focus should be on maintaining jaw position while shaping each pedal note with the tongue. Exercise **4-3** connects the pedal range with the upper register through a descending arpeggio to a pedal tone followed directly by an ascending three octave arpeggio. There is a rest allowing for a breath prior to ascending, but the embouchure should not be reset. The *mf* dynamic should be maintained into the last with a crescendo through the fermata. Three tries maximum is recommended on successfully plan any system. Advanced players may continue the pattern as high as desired and is personally effective.

Section 5 is an adaptation of preface exercises from Walter M. Smith's *Top Tones for the Trumpeter* which were a favorite teaching tool of Don Jacoby. They are notated here at a traditional march tempo and the mental image of playing a march should help with the desired intent. The top note in each case is lengthened from the original in order to focus on centering the pitch. They should be played deliberately and with focus on the articulations and perfectly centered notes while maintaining a *mf* dynamic with little to no crescendo while ascending. Breathing as necessary with three attempts maximum on any system is recommended. Advanced players may continue the pattern as high as desired and personally effective.

The final **Section 6** should be played with careful attention to the notated dynamics. The crescendo while ascending at the top of the exercise should be significant. As in previous exercises, a limit of three attempts to successfully play any system should be the guideline.

Notes

1 COORDINATION

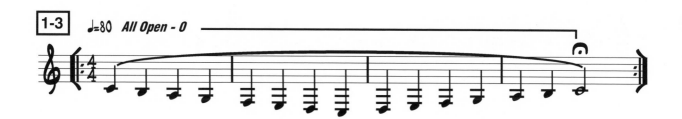

9

2 LONG TONES

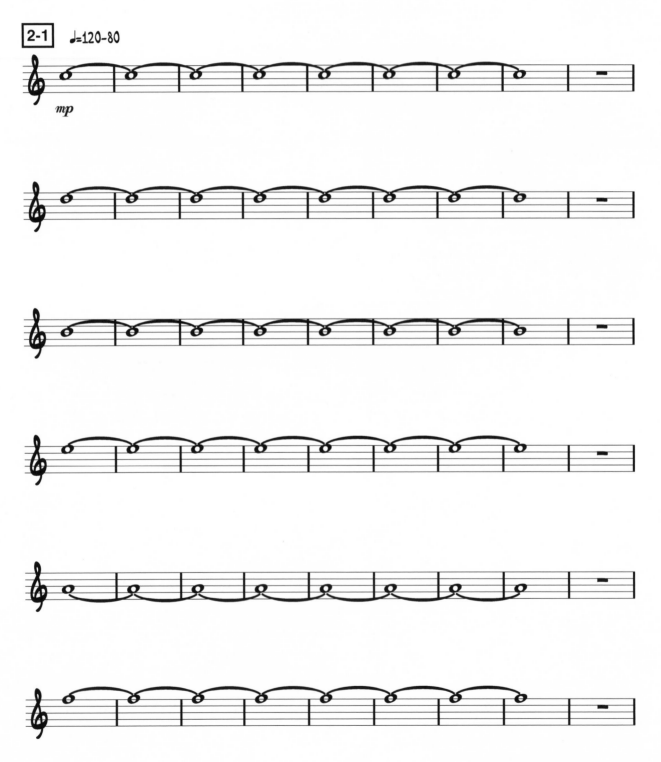

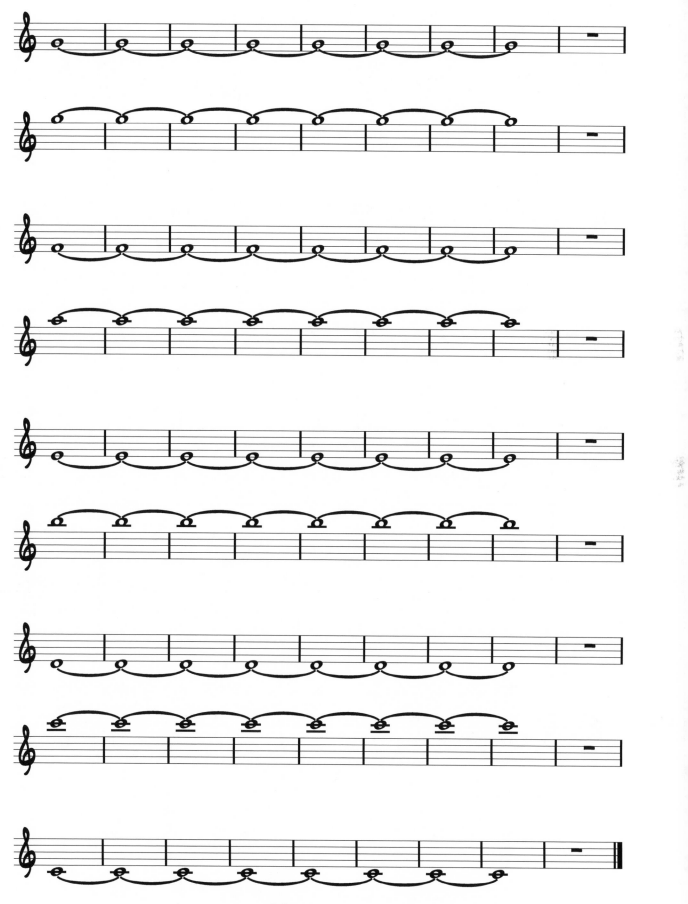

11

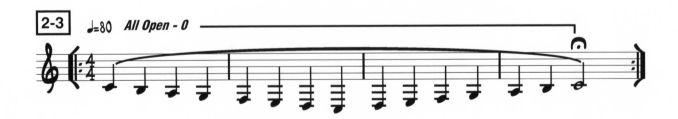

3 FLOW

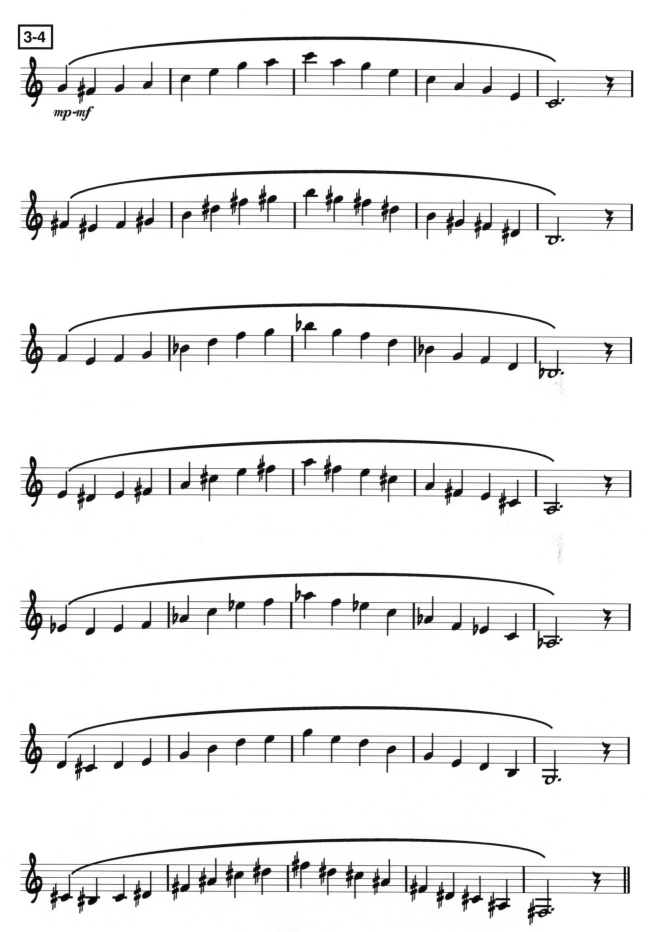

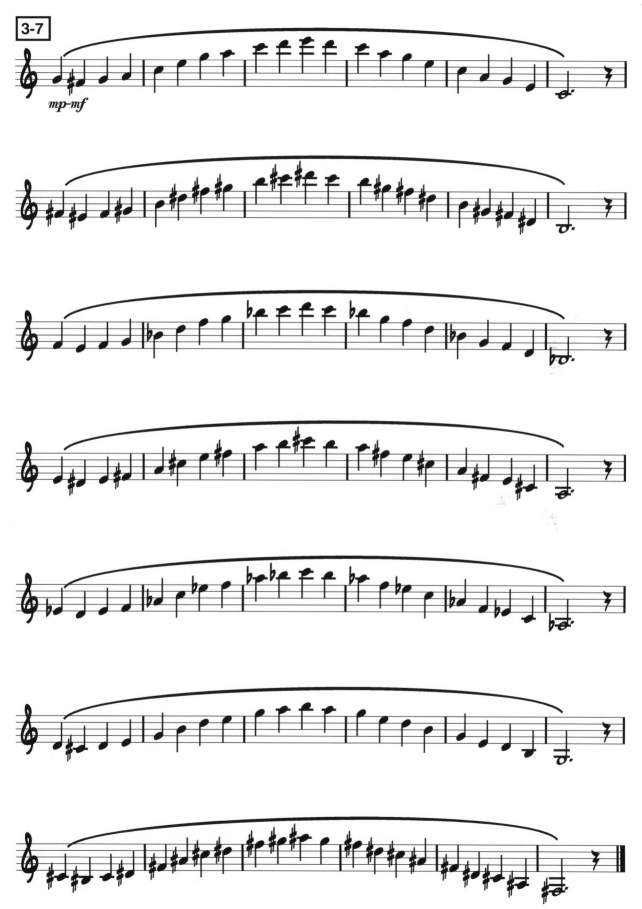

17

18

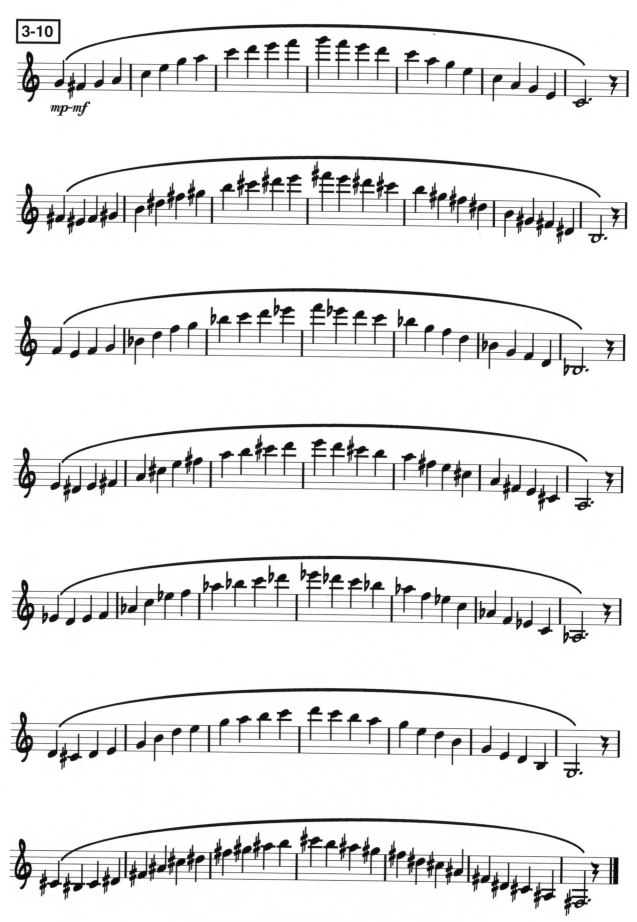

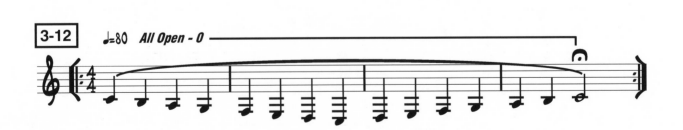

Notes

4 RANGE EXTENSION

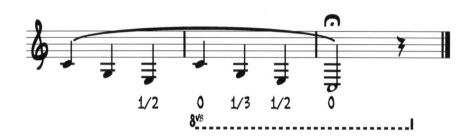

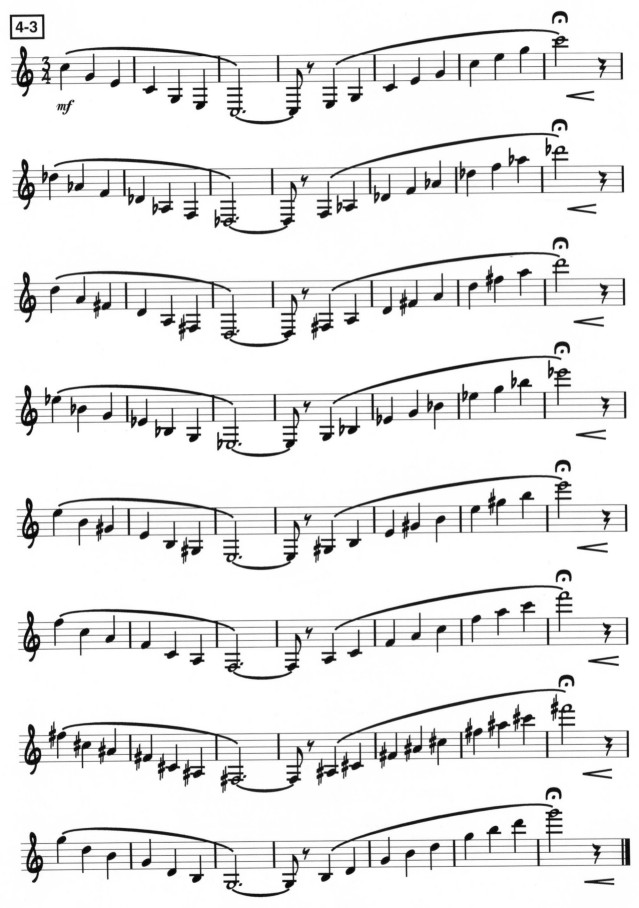

5 ARPEGGIOS WITH ARTICULATIONS

27

Notes

6 ARPEGGIOS WITH RANGE EXTENSION

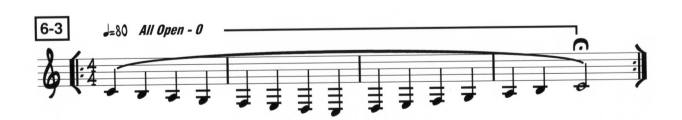

Made in the USA
Monee, IL
19 May 2023

34103574R00020